ADVANCE PRAISE FOR TOTAL INTERNSHIP MANAGEMENT: SUPERVISOR'S HANDBOOK

This handbook is a must read for all internship supervisors. From the day interns arrive, until the day the program wraps up, this handbook provides all of the critical information and techniques needed to ensure a win-win internship experience. Highly recommended!

— Lauren Amershadian, College Recruiting Specialist, Mattel, Inc.

"This handbook covers it all from A-Z and is an extremely valuable resource. Laura offers great advice and guidance for supervisors involved in the launch or improvement of internship programs. This publication offers a fresh prospective on an important investment.....human capital."

— Yvonne Rogers, Relationship and Program Manager, John Hancock

"This handbook is designed to help supervisors effectively guide interns to complete a meaningful internship which meets real needs of students and the organization. A list of potential activities or projects for interns can be customized to meet specific organizational needs and is sure to enhance the quality of the internship experience."

— Dr. Dixie R. Case, Director of Academic Internships, University of Memphis

"Outstanding job on creating a single source for understanding the various components necessary to create a robust internship program. This guide gives a realistic overview of the resources and effort it takes to sustain competitive internship programs. It is a great guide for the company developing a new program and a solid reference for a company like Amway that has over 115 interns"

— Kevin Douglas, College Talent Acquisition Program Manager, Amway

"This is a great self-check for anyone that is thinking about supervising an intern and wants to know how to be most effective. This handbook will equip readers with the necessary knowledge to support their organization's internship program and handle challenges as they occur."

— Greg Muccio, Team Leader People, Southwest Airlines

"I love this handbook! It contains a ton of information that an individual needs to know to be a great internship supervisor. From start to finish, this book covers it all. Great job!"

— Betsy Richards, Director, Career Resources, Kaplan University

Total Internship Management:
Supervisor's Handbook

Laura Szadvari

First Printing

Intern Bridge, Inc.

Total Internship Management:
Supervisor's Handbook

By Laura Szadvari

ISBN 978-0-9799373-7-8

First Printing January 2009

Published by Intern Bridge, Inc.
19 Railroad Street, Suite 3B
Acton, MA 01720

For sales information, please email Sales@InternBridge.com or call us at 800-531-6091.

Cover design/layout/production: bookpackgraphics@yahoo.com (Dan Berger)

Printed in U.S.A.

ABOUT THE AUTHOR

Laura Szadvari has spent the last fourteen years working with college students and their families. A former human resources generalist in the insurance industry with a passion for recruiting, Szadvari moved into a role as a College Recruiter for the Los Angeles branch of a national business and strategy consulting firm. After gaining experience within the wonderful world of college recruiting, she then moved on to become the College Recruiting Manager for the eastern region of a national information and business consulting firm.

Working as an independent consultant for two start-up technology firms wishing to develop and implement a nationally recognized college recruiting program, Szadvari decided that what she loved more than anything was working directly with college students on college campuses. To this effect, she went back to school to pursue a Masters Degree in Education. Throughout graduate school, she worked at The George Washington University where, amongst other things, she managed the Service Learning internship program for all undergraduate students.

After a brief stint as the Princeton Review's Director of Tutoring for the state of Virginia, Szadvari obtained the position of Associate Director of Internships at The University of Mary Washington in Fredericksburg, VA. In addition to managing the internship program on campus, she also assists students with resume and cover letter preparation, interviewing skills, job search strategies, and career counseling.

She has degrees from The University of Pennsylvania and Marymount University and lives outside of the city with her husband and son.

TABLE OF CONTENTS

CHAPTER ONE

GOT INTERNS?

Imagine the following: You've just come out of a planning meeting with your boss where you've been told, "Hey, guess what?! You, my lucky one, are getting an intern next semester!" While your boss happily chatters on about the importance of orientation meetings, learning goals and objectives, performance evaluations, and mentorship, you sit quietly, wringing your sweaty hands in anxiety. You walk out of the office in a daze, alternating between anger ("I don't have time for this!"), confusion ("What am I supposed to do with an intern?"), fear ("What if I screw this up?"), and tempered excitement ("I guess this could, maybe, be good—right?"). As the starting date draws closer, you continue to wait for some guidance from your boss or, at the very least, from your Human Resources Department. But, alas, none comes. The next thing you know, you are shaking hands with a very nice but seemingly inexperienced college student who is looking to you for all the answers.

Sound familiar?

You may not have experienced this exact situation, but if you are reading this handbook you are, no doubt, in need of some assistance. Perhaps you are an inexperienced supervisor unfamiliar with the world of internships? Maybe you are a veteran director in need of an intern refresher course? Or perchance you are a superstar small business owner new to the world of employee, much less intern, management? Whatever your qualifications (or lack thereof), this handbook is designed to help you navigate the world of internships, focusing specifically on how you, as an intern supervisor, can create an extraordinary win-win situation for both your company and your intern. It can be done and the results ***can*** be extraordinary!

However, before delving into specific supervisory techniques and precise management methods, it is necessary to (re)examine the basics: what are internships? Why are they important? Where and when do they take place, and who is involved in the process? And most importantly, how does this affect you?

THE BASICS

Internships are short-term, on-the-job learning experiences designed to allow students to apply knowledge gained in the classroom to a real-world, professional work setting. These work experiences may be paid or unpaid, for academic credit or not for credit, full-time or part-time. Typically, students will complete an internship in a field related to their major, but this is not always the case. While summer internships tend to be the most popular, fall and spring internship opportunities are plentiful and generally easier to obtain. The role the student assumes within the organization is often one with a fair amount of responsibility, especially if the student is an upperclassman. Usually, there is also an educational component to the experience via assigned papers, projects, or readings from a faculty advisor. The student learns through observation, participation, and reflection on what occurred during both the work experience and the concurrent academic experience.

Although some schools require their students to complete internships during the course of their college education, many students complete internships voluntarily because they want to build their resumes and, quite possibly, make contacts for a future full-time job search. Many students will choose to intern at several different places, which is beneficial, even necessary, in today's tight job market. Interning allows students to learn new skills and develop their personal and professional interests. The opportunity helps students better understand particular fields of interest by exposing them to new information and knowledge in a non-classroom setting which, in turn, prepares them for a more effective transition into a career.

In the last several years, companies ranging from *Fortune* 500 giants to "mom-and-pop" start-ups have begun to realize that it makes strategic business sense to align their hiring goals with the experiential learning opportunities that they, themselves, can provide. College students can be very enthusiastic, highly capable, and extremely valuable contributors to an organization's mission if the internship program is well planned and well executed. Interns often possess subject-specific knowledge and technical skills that full-time employees do not. In addition, these students can bring in a fresh, structured approach to business that is not always evident in more seasoned employees. In fact, for many companies, student interns are vital to their long-term success; internship programs are a wonderful recruiting tool as well as a demonstrated way to test out potential full-time, permanent employees. Former student interns who are successfully converted to full-time status often have minimal learning curves and an easier time acclimating to a company's culture.

Ideally, the internship experience should be a win-win situation for both students and employers. Students should be able to view the internship experience as a career opportunity (and not just a semester-long job) on their path towards graduation, while employers should be able to view the internship experience as an opportunity to utilize the skills, talents, and insight of enthusiastic, motivated young professionals with fresh outlooks and creative, out-of-the-box ideas. The opportunity to "try before you buy" is a huge advantage to both students and employers. If things don't work out on either end, either party can choose not to pursue a further relationship, no strings attached. And, conversely, if the internship experience is successful, regardless of what the future brings, students will walk away with a renewed sense of confidence, competence, and self-awareness, and the company will develop (or maintain) a stellar reputation that is sure to foster good will with other top-notch students on campus.

However, the internship relationship between student and company is not always as romantic as it sounds. Not all companies are suitable for internships, and the experience can potentially backfire without the proper preparations in place. Programs that are not implemented well can be, at best, ineffective for the company and, at worst, detrimental to the intern. And that's where you come in. The intern manager or supervisor is a key figure in the life of the intern and can easily be the most influential factor in determining whether the experience is a good one or a bad one. As a result, it is imperative that the individual in charge of the intern feels confident with his or her role. And, as any successful manager will tell you, planning (and, of course, practice) makes perfect.

PLEASE REMEMBER:

- ❖ It is okay if you are not familiar with the world of internships or simply need a refresher course – this book will help.
- ❖ Internships can be extremely beneficial to both the student and the organization.
- ❖ Planning for the internship is critical to ensuring a great experience.

CHAPTER TWO

ALL THE WORLD'S A STAGE (AND YOU'RE THE ONLY PLAYER!)

Actually, that is not entirely true. You are not the only player. In order to create a valuable internship experience for both the student and the organization, there has to be a company-wide commitment in place. Every member of the business, from the CEO to the administrative assistant, needs to understand that he or she plays a very important role in the success of the internship program. However, as the direct supervisor of the intern, you are, in fact, the *most* important player. How you view the internship at the get-go will, for better or worse, influence how well your program works and how effective the experience is for all involved. So, with that in mind, let's discuss how to plan for your intern, or how to "set the stage" for the next few months.

ADJUSTING YOUR ATTITUDE

For just a moment, let's briefly revisit the benefits of an internship from both the student and employer perspectives.

The student chooses to complete an internship in order to:

- Learn as much as possible about a particular field or industry in a professional work setting;
- Perform a variety of tasks that are not available to the student via the classroom;
- Make personal contacts and connections for future networking purposes;
- Build a professional portfolio of materials and resources.

The employer chooses to sponsor an internship in order to:

- Obtain a source of new ideas, fresh outlooks, and creative solutions;
- Build a recruiting pipeline for future needs;

❖ Expand the organization's capacity for growth and development;

❖ Provide a method of completing projects that have been on the "back burner";

❖ Develop a favorable image and reputation on campus.

A bonus to companies is that those students who participate in internships and are consequently hired full-time usually perform better and stay longer than candidates who are hired directly from campus or the open market.

Though it sounds like a wonderful, complementary relationship, the idea of hosting a student intern can be a bit scary for many managers. These young students, so eager to learn, can take up valuable time; they ask questions, require training, and need mentoring. While they are usually very intelligent and capable, they aren't always business savvy. They may not understand the concept of "business casual", might see nothing wrong with whipping out their cell phone to text message their friends, and could very well view an hour-long conversation about the newest MTV reality show as perfectly appropriate. Students have lots of competing priorities and may have to modify their internship hours to accommodate class exams, sports practices, and extracurricular club meetings. They may well have "book" knowledge, but lack common sense. Sounds overwhelming, doesn't it? However, all of these concerns aside, students are, by far, one of the most enthusiastic, passionate groups of workers in the marketplace and, with the right manager in place, they can add tremendous support to any organization willing to make the proper investment.

The most important thing that you need to know, first and foremost, is that providing a successful experience requires a fair amount of time and effort. If you understand this fact up front, and will yourself to accept it, you are ahead of the game. The simple fact is that an internship program that is poorly thought out has the potential to fail, and the manager who believes that you can throw an intern into a "sink or swim" situation on day one will most likely come to regret this decision by day two. Remember that we are living in an age in which you can reach millions of people with a single click of a mouse. Students know how to do this better than anyone. With the advent of social networking sites like MySpace and Facebook, the endless number of online blogging sites and semi-professional "chat" boards, and the myriad of students' own personal web pages, a single negative comment about a company can cause serious harm to its reputation at several college campuses and with several hundred students simultaneously! Students are not shy. They are just as likely to brag about great experiences as they are to complain about horrible ones. To protect your company's professional branding, and to maintain the wonderful image which (I'm sure) you deserve, take care to think through, plan out, and structure the experience accordingly.

You should be committed to spending some energy orienting, training, mentoring, and evaluating the student throughout the entire course of the internship if you want it to be effective. Consider yourself a teacher, and use this role to your advantage. Shape the internship to meet your needs, but make sure that you are providing a quality learning experience for the student. Remember that the student may be working for little or no compensation, so it is imperative that he or she obtains relevant, marketable experience that will pay off later on down the road. View the process as a strategic instrument in your management toolkit. Not only are you honing your own supervisory skills, but, from a larger, more corporate perspective, you are facilitating a long-term investment in your company's business practices and culture. Think about what you want to get from the program, and then use these goals to develop learning objectives for the student (more on this later). At some point, every business professional has uttered the phrase, "I wish I knew then what I know now." Try to recall what you wish you had been taught, and pass that knowledge on to your student. The reward system inherent in internship programs is actually very simple: more sharing leads to more learning, which, in turn, leads to a better program which, inevitably, leads to better candidates. And then the cycle repeats itself, over and over. While it may appear that experienced supervisors will have an easier time managing an intern, inexperienced supervisors can do just as good a job if they use some basic common sense and follow some very simply guidelines: make interns feel like part of the team, emphasize the significance of their contribution, provide a variety of interesting and meaningful tasks, answer questions, provide feedback, and never, ever treat students like second-class citizens.

In a nutshell, internship programs, like most everything else in life, are largely what you make of them. If you view the experience as a burden, it is going to be a burden. If you see the student as nothing more than a kid who needs something to do, you are setting yourself (and the innocent intern) up for failure. If you think that the internship is merely an opportunity to get free labor, you are not only exploiting the student but also doing irreparable harm to your company and it's reputation on campus (remember, students talk!). As the intern's supervisor and main point of contact, you have much to do with the student having either a positive or negative experience—the biggest (and most significant) factor under your control is your attitude. Make it a positive one and everybody wins.

INVOLVING YOUR TEAM

Whether you may have volunteered or were chosen to be the internship supervisor, it is vital that you remember to involve your team (and, in fact, your entire company) in the intern-employer relationship. The internship will be a much better and more well-rounded experience for the student if he or she has other employees aside from you to interact with. Everybody has a story to tell, and let's be honest: people like to talk about themselves! By encouraging your staff members to share their stories, suggestions, and words of wisdom with the intern, you are not only enabling the student to obtain more information about the industry, but also allowing your staff the opportunity to informally mentor and/or coach a member of the upcoming workforce. What a value-added opportunity for everyone! To take this concept one step further, you might want to consider using the internship as a means to reward your best employees. Ask them to provide shadowing experiences, request that they take the intern out to lunch (on the company dime, of course!), solicit their ideas and suggestions in regard to intern training and professional development, or have them staff "lunch and learns" on specific topics of interest. Including others in your internship program will benefit the intern and allow your employees to further develop their own professional competencies.

Ideally, the internship program should be a collaborative effort between you, your team, and the student. All employees should make a concerted effort to make the intern feel welcome and comfortable and should provide the intern with guidance and direction. If increased productivity is one of your goals for the experience (as it should be), it should be made absolutely clear to your staff that the intern is not there to do work that others are trying to avoid. In other words, no scut work allowed! However, because the intern will undoubtedly value the opportunity to learn from others, you might want to consider asking a few select employees to provide you with one or two projects with which they need help. Understand and explain to others that any work assigned to the intern should be impressive enough for use on the student's resume. Working as a team, you can brainstorm how these projects would benefit the intern and how the chain of management should work. If you are so inclined, this might even be a great chance for you to start developing your junior-level supervisors into senior level managers!

Despite the fact that you are the lead actor in this drama, you do have a supporting cast. Speak positively to your team about the internship program, introduce them to the student, welcome their suggestions, and listen to their concerns. And bear in mind that, while your working relationship with the intern may last only a few months, your professional connection to your team may last for years, so you want to do what you can to foster these relationships.

PREPARING THE WORKSPACE

Yes, this may seem like a no-brainer, but please remember that your intern needs to have an actual space in which to work! Plopping a laptop down in the middle of the floor next to a stack of post-it notes and a pencil is hardly an appropriate accommodation. At the very least, you should have arrangements in place for a desk, chair, telephone, computer, and various office supplies before the intern shows up for his or her first day of work. Staging a proper orientation for the intern will be discussed in a subsequent chapter, but just know for now that if you want your intern to feel like a valued contributor to your company, you must provide the tools required for the student to be successful.

PLEASE REMEMBER:

- ❖ Supervising an intern can be challenging at times, but maintaining a positive attitude will help to make the experience much more manageable and rewarding.
- ❖ While you are playing the lead role in this experience, look to your fellow employees as your supporting cast members. Involving the others on your team will help to make the internship experience much more well-rounded for your intern and will allow your employees to hone their interpersonal skills.
- ❖ Make sure that your student has the necessary supplies to start being productive on the very first day of the internship.

CHAPTER THREE

BE ALL THAT YOU CAN BE (AS AN INTERNSHIP SUPERVISOR)

It can be daunting to be an internship supervisor. You are required to be the intern's day-to-day manager, but also expected to provide for the intern's teaching, mentoring, coaching, counseling, and advocating. Due to the fact that college students require more attention than do experienced business professionals, you will find that your role is multi-faceted and that you will need to shift amongst these roles throughout the course of the semester. While there are definitely traits that supervisors of interns and supervisors of seasoned employees seem to share, do not be fooled into thinking that these positions are one and the same. In fact, internship supervisors need to possess certain unique characteristics that fall outside of the typical "manager" job description. Let's briefly explore the makeup of an ideal internship supervisor.

First and foremost, the intern's supervisor should be an individual who is physically available to the student on a day-to-day basis. Student interns cannot be expected to possess the same level of autonomy as experienced business professionals, and will therefore need frequent monitoring, especially in the beginning of the internship. On-going supervision of this kind is essential to a successful experience. You must remember that the professional business world is quite different from the academic collegiate world, especially in regard to clarity of goals and expectations and regularity of feedback. Undergraduate students are accustomed to working under professors who clearly and specifically delineate what the students' responsibilities are and the timeline under which these tasks must be completed. Throughout a course, professors provide consistent advice and make themselves available to answer questions and address concerns. As a result, students expect and appreciate clear direction regarding their work and continual evaluations (both informal and formal) concerning what they have done and how well they have done it.

One of the major responsibilities of the ideal internship supervisor is to help the student create a bridge between the college world and the workplace by providing unambiguous instructions, constructive feedback, and time for reflection. Again, this is most crucial during the early stages of the internship when many students will be anxious, shy, confused, and even intimidated by even the most gentle of bosses. An easy way to accomplish this kind of communication is to set up a regular time, on a weekly basis, to meet with your intern. Half an hour, or an hour at most, will allow your student the opportunity to discuss any questions or concerns and alleviate the potential fear that he or she is not performing up to par. We will address evaluations in more detail in a later chapter.

Another trait that all internship supervisors should share is having specific expertise in the area in which the intern is working. This may sound obvious, but believe me when I say that I have seen some excellent, very high-level "subject-matter expert" managers try to manage student interns who were working in areas completely foreign to them. These managers were chosen to supervise the interns because of their expert interpersonal skills and "warm and fuzzy" attitudes (both of which are important); however, because of their lack of knowledge in their interns' area of work, they could not contribute to meeting the interns' learning goals. This, obviously, was a real problem. Supervisors (and the staffing managers who assign them) need to remember that internships are very often credit-based. This academic credit is typically awarded on the basis of time spent working at the internship site, as well as the successful completion of academic requirements assigned by a faculty advisor. Learning, and not simply working for the sake of working, is at the heart of all internships—if there is no mechanism in place in which a student can learn (and, by extension, be taught), then the internship experience will be inevitably unsuccessful. Now, to be fair, the intern's supervisor does not necessarily need to be a professor akin to a university faculty member. Still, he or she should be selected or assigned to an intern because he or she likes to teach or train and *has the skills and resources to do it well.*

In some internship programs, the student will come to the site with learning goals and objectives already pre-determined. The responsibility of the internship supervisor will be to provide the intern with tasks that allow him or her to fulfill the requirements of the learning plan. In other internship programs, the supervisor may be required to collaborate with the student to help design these learning goals and objectives. The internship supervisor might also work directly with the student's faculty sponsor to make sure that the learning plan is comprehensive in scope and realistic in practice. Either way, it is vital that the individual supervising the intern has a definitive understanding of the student's field of study, so much so that he or she can discuss progress and performance goals, point out mistakes, assist with solutions, provide praise, evaluate techniques, methods, and procedures, indicate areas of strengths and weaknesses, and suggest resources to further aid in theoretical and/or practical exploration of the field.

Another essential characteristic of a successful internship supervisor is the desire to work with college students. Even though it may not be politically correct to admit this, not all managers have an interest in working with individuals as young and inexperienced as college juniors and seniors. More experienced managers may not have the strong reserves of patience and compassion needed to oversee a student. Nor might they have the dynamic interpersonal and communication skills necessary to interact with college students. Consider that, in college, students are taught how to think critically. Among other things, critical thinking involves questioning assumptions, standards, and beliefs about the world and environment. Students are asked to analyze information, critique it, and suggest methods for improvement. Change is the operative word, and keeping an open mind is fundamental to the learning process. These behaviors, while encouraged and respected in the classroom, are not necessarily desired in the workplace, especially among more conservative, structured organizations. A highly proficient intern manager will understand this difference and work closely with the student to align expectations accordingly and encourage him or her to develop professional human relation skills and political office etiquette.

The internship supervisor serves many roles, most notably boss, teacher, critic, and coach. Although the idea of mentoring will be addressed in a separate chapter of this handbook, suffice it to say that a really great supervisor will share with the student, honestly and realistically, the pros and cons of the industry, and assess his or her capabilities for success. He or she will facilitate networking with others in the industry (a skill at which most students are, sadly, inept) and assist with furthering the student intern's professional competence and confidence. By helping the student to connect theory to practice, the ideal internship supervisor should act as a role model by educating, supporting, and leading the student toward future academic and career success.

PLEASE REMEMBER:

- ❖ Internship supervisors require a different set of skills than do supervisors of more experienced employees.

- ❖ Student interns need assistance bridging the gap between school and work and require close supervision, time for reflection, and a clear explanation of what is expected of them.

- ❖ Internship supervisors should enjoy working with college students and should have an excellent operational knowledge of the subject matter the intern will be working with.

- ❖ There are many roles that internship supervisors assume, including teacher, coach, advocate, and critic. These roles may change often throughout the course of the semester.

CHAPTER FOUR

ALL ABOARD!
CREATING A FIRST CLASS ORIENTATION

By now you should realize that, in order to have a successful internship experience, it is best to carefully prepare ahead of time. Failure to plan is a plan for failure. Each hour spent planning is worth two hours saved during implementation. The seven P's, the six P's, or euphemistically, the five P's (Poor Planning Promotes Poor Performance)...well, you get the idea. The easiest thing to plan for, and yet the one programmatic element overlooked by most employers, is the student intern's orientation to the company. This initial introduction can take place over one day or one week, can be formal or informal, but it is imperative that it happen shortly after the intern starts work. And by shortly, I mean the very first day (or very soon thereafter)! Ideally, you should orient your intern to your company much as you would orient any new full-time member of your staff.

However, I would argue that it is even *more* important that you provide your student intern with a proper orientation. Most college students are not familiar with a professional business environment, so they are (quite understandably) bound to be overwhelmed, intimidated and maybe even downright scared. A main goal of the orientation process is to help alleviate the intern's concerns and to make him or her more at ease in your office setting. Facilitating the transition between college and work will lead to a quicker assimilation, a shorter learning curve, and a much more industrious intern. Making the student feel secure and comfortable will not only assuage their apprehension, but also showcase your hospitality and thoughtfulness. Remember, for better or worse, first impressions count, so you might as well make yours an outstanding one!

UMMM...WHERE IS THE BATHROOM?

While it may seem, at first glance, somewhat trivial to make it a point to tour the restroom facilities at your company, it is actually very important to provide just this sort of basic information to your student intern. You want the intern to feel at home in your business environment. Students are nervous enough about the actual work expected from them, and having to worry about finding the bathroom—or the copy room, or the coffee room—will needlessly contribute to their discomfort. Want to know the easiest way to cover the physical groundwork of your office space? Provide a facility tour! Depending on how large your office is, this can be a quick and dirty ten-minute excursion or a longer, more formal hour-long journey.

However you choose to structure your tour, make sure to cover the following important areas:

- ❖ Intern work space (office, cubicle, etc.)
- ❖ Restrooms
- ❖ Office supply room/copy center
- ❖ Library or reference room (if intern is expected to conduct research)
- ❖ Lunch/break room, cafeteria, or vending machine/watercooler area
- ❖ Parking facilities
- ❖ Fire exits/safety protocol
- ❖ Human Resources office

WHO ARE YOU, AGAIN?

If time permits, a very valuable and considerate thing to do along your tour is to stop and introduce your intern to other members of your team, especially those with whom your intern may be working closely with at some point. This process allows the intern to become familiar with many other friendly faces that he or she can go to with questions and provides a means of establishing rapport and making connections—two important elements necessary for a harmonious working environment. To take this concept one step further, a wonderful idea (if time and scheduling permit) is to secure a personal welcome from a "higher-up" in the company, like the COO, CEO, or President. Want to go crazy? Have that individual present the intern with a welcome gift, like a plant, a cookie arrangement, or a company coffee cup. Your intern will appreciate this more than you will know. Another great idea is to take the intern out to lunch that very first day. Asking the younger members of your team or alumni from the intern's school to join you will probably make the intern more relaxed. Some companies make "lunch and learns" a regular part of their intern program and sponsor weekly lunch programs where different members of the organization meet with the intern over lunch and talk about their particular roles in the company. This works well for companies who have large intern programs, but can work just as easily for the small company with only one student. The point here is that face time does matter, and students are very impressed with companies who put forth the effort to make them feel welcome and involved.

LOSE THE PIERCINGS AND DITCH THE IM'S

During your orientation with your student intern, you should address the norms, values, and work customs that are acceptable in the office. These things will largely depend on your corporate culture and environment. If you work in a more creative field, it may be perfectly acceptable to come to work with facial piercings and tattoos in full public view. If you work in a more conservative area, these things may be forbidden. Some office settings (especially those with heavy client contact) may require formal business dress, while other, more casual settings may be fine with polo shirts and khakis. Again, remember that this may be the very first time your student has worked in a professional business setting. He or she may not have a firm grasp on basic protocol and business etiquette. It is your responsibility, as the intern's supervisor, to help your intern understand what is acceptable and what is not.

During this discussion, you should address the following topics:

- ❖ Dress code / Appearance
- ❖ Internet / Facebook or MySpace / Instant Messaging
- ❖ Cell Phone / Texting

You (or the appropriate Human Resources representative) should also have a conversation with your intern about company-specific issues like attendance, harassment, disciplinary policies, confidentiality codes, and safety measures. It is critical to bear in mind that not all students are alike. In addition to varying degrees of work experience and professional knowledge, your students will also differ in regard to cultural background, learning style, social awareness, emotional maturity, and political and business savior-faire. Err on the conservative side, and protect both the student and your company by providing the same information to every student regardless of what you "think" they already know.

THE DOWN AND DIRTY

How many of us have shown up for the first day at a new job, eager and enthusiastic, ready to take the world by storm, only to find that we can't log in to our computer, our voicemail isn't set up, the copy machine won't work unless provided with a special code, and the security guard wants to make a citizen's arrest because we don't have the appropriate company ID? Probably all of us! And I think we would all agree that the experience was really crummy. To prevent this, do what you can to successfully manage the intern's experience right from the start. Work with your technology department to get user names and passwords established, collaborate with your Human Resources department to secure a parking pass and company ID, and provide your intern with a list of access codes and the necessary instructions for office equipment. If you aren't able to make all of these things happen by day one (and you may, in fact, lack the means to do so), it is not the end of the world as long as you communicate to the intern that you are working on making his or her transition as seamless as possible and will try your best to make these things happen quickly.

THE 411

When students are hired into a company as interns, they are not always provided with specific information about the type of work they will be doing. Neither are they always given in-depth, comprehensive information about the company they will be working for. As part of the orientation process, you should aim to provide to the student both general and specific information about the company, the department, the team, and the specific projects for which the intern will be responsible.

The Big Picture

Try to cover most, if not all, of the following details during your talk:

<u>Information about your company:</u>

- How it was created/founded
- The mission or values statement and accompanying goals
- The products and/or services offered
- The target market/client base
- The competition
- The short and long term growth plans

- ❖ The organizational structure, including the roles and responsibilities of each department or team

Providing the intern with marketing collateral, an organizational chart, and a company directory would be a very nice gesture and would also serve as a point of reference for the student throughout the internship.

The Small Picture

This is the time to talk about the details. Together with the student, you should discuss and agree upon a learning plan for the internship (more on this later).

Be sure to hit on the following points:

- ❖ A clear list of objectives and goals that are SMART (specific, measurable, attainable, realistic, and timely)

- ❖ The projects, tasks, and assignments (and accompanying deadlines) the intern will be required to complete to meet the aforementioned goals

- ❖ All tools and resources available to the student, including other staff members

- ❖ Methods of supervisor evaluation and feedback (informal and formal)

- ❖ Expectations of both supervisor and intern

- ❖ Opportunities for professional development and continued training for the student

- ❖ What to do and where to go for help

Creating and implementing a thorough orientation is one of the best ways to welcome your student intern and to make an excellent first impression. An effective orientation is the foundation upon which a successful internship experience will take root and, I guarantee you, your student will express his or her gratitude—not only through words, but also through a stellar performance.

PLEASE REMEMBER:

❖ Internship supervisors require a different set of skills than do supervisors of more experienced employees.

❖ No matter how big or small your facility, a tour is always a good idea.

CHAPTER FIVE

INTERNSHIPS: THE NEXT GENERATION

Gone are the days when having an intern meant relegating him or her to getting coffee, making copies, and sorting mail. Of course, these tasks may still be a part of an internship experience, but, certainly, they should not be the only duties involved. Today's college students crave responsibility and autonomy. We hear about this generation of students, the *millennials*, wanting to make a contribution to, and make a difference in, society.

Translated into internship-speak, this means, for example, writing a financial plan that will affect a company's bottom line, producing a marketing strategy that will conquer a particular target segment, or creating a website that will forge the company's transition into the e-commerce market. These students don't want to do meaningless work for which there is 1) no relevance to their field of study, 2) no connection to the company's mission, and 3) no reason a trained monkey could not perform in their place! As a supervisor, it is critical that you understand that not only do these students expect meaningful work (and a lot of it!), they also *crave* it. Remember, students are participating in an internship so they can gain professional, real-world experience in a particular area of interest. Internships are meant to be a learning experience for the student, and, unfortunately, faxing documents, working the switchboard, and filing invoices don't qualify as such. In fact, most university internship programs will not allow a company to post an internship listing with their school if the position is more than 20% - 30% clerical in nature.

As an internship supervisor, you must think very carefully as you create (or refine, if the position was created by someone other than you) the internship opportunity you have available.

There are two main things to think about here:
1) the actual internship **job description** that you will post with the school and;

2) the specific internship **learning objectives** that you will create in conjunction with the student (and/or faculty advisor if he or she is involved).

THE JOB DESCRIPTION

Creating a proper internship job description is one of the key factors to internship program success. First and foremost, one of your main goals as an internship provider is to create a plan that adequately provides for the work your company needs accomplished. Additionally, the job description must be attractive to the student, in that it allows for the opportunity to learn about the specific nature of your business. You want to provide a variety of tasks for the student to perform (thus alleviating boredom and creating a dynamic experience), but each and every one of these duties should be a "resume-worthy" item. In other words, any major project that you assign to an intern should be something that he or she could put on a resume to illustrate significant work experience and/or industry exposure.

The best way to create an internship job description is by thinking about the kinds of tasks that you would want an intern to complete. Each component of the description should be clearly defined and easily manageable. Ideally, each responsibility should be beneficial to the intern and meaningful to the company. While interns expect that their work will be challenging, you should ensure that the proper resources exist for the student to successfully achieve the goal. A great internship experience will consist of a nice balance of independent work and teamwork. As well, you should include tasks of differing length, some that are short-term (can be finished in a few hours to a few days), and some that are long-term (to be completed over the course of the internship). These longer-term projects will serve to keep the intern busy in the event of some unanticipated down time. As your interns progress through the semester, you will undoubtedly notice that they become more and more confident and capable. It is not a bad idea to structure your internship so that the intern is assigned more complex work in the final couple of months. By that time, he or she will have learned about both your industry in general and your business in particular, and will have a good knowledge of the tools and resources available at your company that can be used to get tasks completed. Remember, variety is the spice of life (and students sometimes have short attention spans!), so be sure to provide for a plethora of activities to stimulate their minds and channel their energy.

Since the job description is essentially a written summary of the internship opportunity, it should be realistic and legitimate. In other words, although roles and responsibilities oftentimes are "revised" during the course of the semester, the job description should be your best, most accurate guess at what the intern will actually be doing. Pulling a "bait–and-switch" by making the internship sound much better than it will actually be is not only unfair and unethical, but will also buy you a very unfavorable reputation on campus! In a nutshell, in order for the student to be a productive member of your staff, he or she must clearly understand the duties you have assigned and the expectations you have created. This information can and should be found on the job posting you have produced. Please keep in mind that not only do students want to utilize the skills in which they are strong, they also want to further develop the areas in which they are weak. This will be discussed in more detail in the following section on learning objectives.

Depending on the nature of your business and the type of student intern you are seeking to hire, the following are a list of potential assignment "openers" you may want to consider.

Please note that these are very general, open-ended ideas intended to be made more specific by you and/or your team and that this list is ***by no means*** exhaustive.

- ❖ Write a manual/handbook
- ❖ Design a website
- ❖ Research a topic and prepare a presentation
- ❖ Create a lesson and conduct a training/educational session
- ❖ Plan an event
- ❖ Build or update a database
- ❖ Revise/revamp a system
- ❖ Conduct a study/experiment
- ❖ Compile a benchmarking analysis
- ❖ Plan and implement a marketing campaign
- ❖ Participate in a team project
- ❖ Develop a list of potential sponsors/funding sources
- ❖ Perform software programming or hardware maintenance
- ❖ Prepare a report
- ❖ Visit a client/attend a meeting or a conference
- ❖ Design a newsletter
- ❖ Assemble a portfolio
- ❖ Create an archive
- ❖ Identify business opportunities
- ❖ Monitor news
- ❖ Organize documents
- ❖ Interview individuals and write up a summary of responses/an article

- ❖ Analyze and sort data
- ❖ Produce a film
- ❖ Translate materials
- ❖ Map and record data
- ❖ Investigate a scenario
- ❖ Prepare a response
- ❖ Undergo training
- ❖ Process tax returns/reconcile bank statements
- ❖ Develop a survey

IMPORTANT NOTE!

As you are putting together the different projects that will comprise your job description, please remember that each project should have a specified start- and end-date, as well as a means of evaluation. We will discuss methods of assessment in a separate chapter, but for now just understand that you will need to provide feedback to the intern for each task that he or she completes. Methods of feedback will vary.

LEARNING OBJECTIVES

Learning objectives are brief, clear, succinct statements of what an individual will learn as a result of performing specific tasks or activities. With regard to internships, these goals typically fall into four different categories:

1) Particular skill development,
2) General academic enrichment,
3) Career exploration and examination, and
4) Personal improvement and enhancement.

In a perfect internship, each learning objective the student has in mind will directly correlate to a specific assignment delegated by you, the supervisor. Therefore, the student will meet each learning objective by the fulfillment of a certain job task. But we all know that perfection doesn't happen often, so instead, let's talk about reality!

At most universities, internship agreements involve a three-party contractual agreement amongst the school, the student, and the site. In the majority of cases, although certainly not always, students work concurrently with faculty

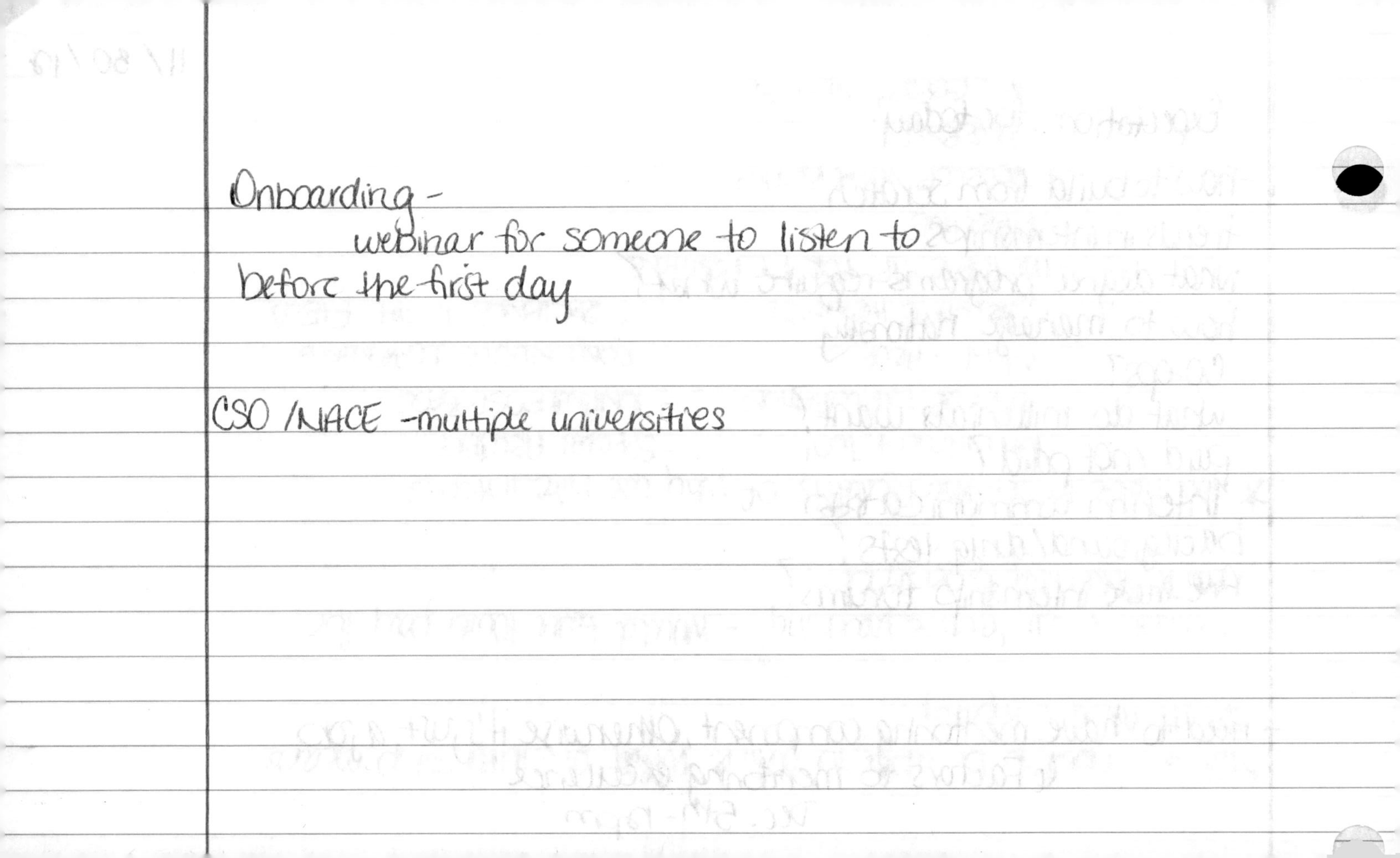

Onboarding -
webinar for someone to listen to
before the first day

CSO / NACE - multiple universities

advisors at the same time that they work with you. Best care scenarios dictate that the intern will have already created a set of learning objectives with his or her faculty advisor. In this instance, it is up to you to discuss these learning objectives with the student soon after the internship begins so that you and the student can jointly determine via which assignments these objectives can be met. Hopefully, the job description you created during the internship planning process will allow the intern to meet his or her goals. If not, you will want to revise or tweak some or all of the tasks in order to meet the student's learning aspirations. In the event that the student enters into the internship without a pre-determined set of learning objectives, it is up to you, the supervisor, to sit down and brainstorm with the intern and determine how best to create such a learning plan. Using the previously constructed job description should guide you in this endeavor.

Learning objectives, whether created between the student and the faculty advisor, the student and the internship supervisor, or amongst all three parties, will serve to identify, describe, and structure the knowledge gained through the internship. In creating or reviewing such a plan, a few questions need to be asked. Firstly, it is important to think about what learning goals are possible to obtain in the time frame of an internship (typically fourteen to sixteen weeks). Secondly, what tools and resources will the intern have at his or her disposal to accomplish such objectives? Thirdly, what methods of evaluation exist to determine whether or not the expectations have been met? As a supervisor, you may have heard about the S.M.A.R.T. goal system. To briefly review (or for you first-timers), when setting goals for yourself or for others, you must remember to make the goals:

1) Specific (who, what, where, when, why),

2) Measurable (there must be a concrete method of evaluating success),

3) Attainable (both small goals as well as larger ones),

4) Realistic (are there appropriate resources in place to support success?), and

5) Timely (firm starting and ending dates). These same guidelines apply to creating learning objectives for interns.

Remember, students will have unique reasons for wanting to participate in internships. They will also differ in what strengths they bring to the table and in what areas they want to work on improving. Therefore, no two learning plans will be the same (although two students may share one or more individual objectives). While we will discuss feedback and evaluation methods in a subsequent chapter, please note that as the student progresses through the internship, you will be periodically reviewing his or her work. You and the student may very well find that a learning objective has not been met by a particular project and, therefore, another task needs to be assigned. This is okay. Alternatively, you may find that the student mastered an objective much more quickly than anticipated and, therefore, other objectives need to be added. This is fine, as well. Finally, you and the student may realize, as the internship progresses, that learning objectives need to be changed as student interests and/or business priorities shift. No problem. The learning plan should be a working, living document that (assuming all parties are in agreement) has the ability to be adjusted at will.

Internships are designed to enhance and complement a student's formal education in the classroom. Learning objectives that are carefully constructed will ensure that students obtain the best internship experience possible and that employers reap the value of the student's expertise. By providing a well thought-out structure to the internship, learning objectives will increase the productivity of the student in the workplace while, at the same time, enabling the student to successfully achieve his or her aspirations.

The following is a list of sample learning objectives and accompanying learning tasks. Again, please understand that these are very simple examples only and that they are, in large part, generic. They are not intended to be a "catch-all" for the majority of your interns. You will also see that, sometimes, learning objectives and learning tasks may fall within more than one particular area. That is fine. Again, learning plans are not set in stone and must remain, by their very nature, malleable.

AREA 1: PARTICULAR SKILL DEVELOPMENT	
Learning Objective	**Learning Task**
I want to learn how to structure and write a news article.	I will cover the local government elections and publish an article in next Monday's newspaper.
I want to strengthen my use of Microsoft Access.	By February 25th, I will have converted all of our paper client records into electronic form in Microsoft Access.
I want to further develop my public speaking skills and alleviate my anxiety about speaking in front of a crowd.	I will prepare weekly status reports and present them at our team meetings.
AREA 2: GENERAL ACADEMIC ENRICHMENT	
Learning Objective	**Learning Task**
I want to further understand the different medical disorders associated with premature infants.	I will conduct patient rounds with my supervisor, take copious notes, and write a report with my findings by the end of the semester.
I want to elucidate a greater connection between Civil War History and the battlefields of Fredericksburg, VA.	I will explore three battlefields in Fredericksburg, take photos, and compile a collage of names, dates, and events within the next two weeks.
I want to experience sales, specifically cold calling and direct marketing, firsthand.	I will research potential clients, conduct a one-week marathon telephone blitz, and produce a chart that summarizes my results.
AREA 3: CAREER EXPLORATION AND EXAMINATION	
I want to understand more about the field of criminal law.	I will attend at least two courtroom trials over the next four months and interview a prosecuting attorney, a defense attorney, and a judge. I will write a reflective paper on my experience.

(continued on page 36)

AREA 3: CAREER EXPLORATION AND EXAMINATION (CONT.)	
Learning Objective	**Learning Task**
I am pretty sure I want to be an ESL (English as a Second Language) teacher, but I want to learn more about the job first.	As part of my internship, I will spend two hours each week in the classroom assisting a teacher with lesson implementation and providing one-on-one tutoring to individual students.
I want to participate in planning an event from start to finish.	I will work with the Director of Special Events on the annual black-tie gala where my responsibilities will include: compiling the invitation list, securing the space, arranging for food, beverage, decorations, and music, and monitoring the silent auction. ***(Note: This learning task should be subsequently broken down into "sub" learning tasks for each activity mentioned.)***

AREA 4: PERSONAL IMPROVEMENT AND BETTERMENT	
Learning Objective	**Learning Task**
I want to learn how to listen better and interrupt less.	I will conduct informational interviews with three of my team members about their specific roles within the company and write a report that paraphrases their remarks by the end of my internship. ***(Note: This learning task can also cover Area 3 if the intern also wants to find out more about the particular company in which he or she is working.)***
I want to improve my social etiquette skills during mealtime. ***(Note: This learning objective can also be considered within Area 1.)***	I will go out to a sit-down lunch on a weekly basis with someone from my team.

(continued on page 37)

AREA 4: PERSONAL IMPROVEMENT AND BETTERMENT (CONT.)	
Learning Objective	**Learning Task**
I want to obtain better understanding of what "business casual" dress means within my industry.	I will visit different departments within my company and take notes on the different styles I see. I will present a portfolio consisting of pictures (live or from magazines), personal notes, and professional articles to my supervisor by the 4th of November.

A BRIEF DISCUSSION ABOUT THE CURRENT GENERATION OF STUDENTS

This chapter would not be complete without a few additional words about the "millennial" generation of students. As a result of the enormous differences between these individuals and folks already in the workforce, research has been conducted, case studies have been carried out, articles have been written, and books have been published. My intent is not to provide you with a thorough analysis of the differences between generations of workplace employees, but instead to give you an overview of the most important things you need to know about these students in regards to internships.

First and foremost, please understand that I don't believe you can categorize an entire generation of students into one specific stereotype. Not all of today's students will fit into the mold I am about to present.

However, I think that it is still acceptable to base your job descriptions and learning objectives on the following information because, whether or not students typify more or less of the following attributes, using the data below will allow you to create valuable experiences for any students that cross your path.

A SUMMARY

The good:

The millennial generation of students brings with it a set of new values and a new definition of work ethic. Students of this generation (typically those who were born between 1980 and 2000, although depending on with whom you speak, those dates will vary) are big fans of collaboration, structure, risk-taking, and technology. They are sociable, talented, open-minded, and achievement-oriented. These students have very high expectations for themselves and from others. They are quite skilled at time management, multi-tasking, and problem-solving. Students of the millennial generation are tolerant of others, value inclusiveness, and promote multiculturalism and globalism. They enjoy challenge, welcome leadership opportunities, like flexibility, and value respect. In general, their outlook is positive and hopeful.

The not-so-good (but not really bad):

These students expect a lot! While they are generally a fairly optimistic bunch, they are also sometimes impatient when things don't move fast enough or don't entirely meet their expectations. They are used to moving at the speed of light and having been (over)scheduled for much of their lives, but occasionally work so quickly that they miss important details or skim over areas where they should have paid a bit more attention. They are not afraid of taking risks and do not fear making mistakes since they view these occasions as learning opportunities; however, this sometimes leads to carelessness and a lack of due diligence on their part. They are extremely technologically advanced and may not have a lot of tolerance for those who are "out of the loop" or "behind the times". The concept of "paying your dues" may be foreign to these students, especially if they believe (and many of them do) that they are quite capable of jumping into a more complex role from the get go. Tenure does not mean as much to them as credibility; in other words, the fact that an employee has been with a company for ten years does not mean as much as the fact that a relative newbie has a better education and many more creative ideas. Their belief in the concept of "fairness", while admirable, may sometimes not sit well with the managers of more conservative, hierarchically structured companies. Oh yes, and they want to have fun and get paid (really, really well paid!).

WHAT DOES THIS MEAN TO YOU?

Ideally, and as much as possible, you should try to create learning experiences that satisfy the needs and adhere to the values of the millennial generation of students.

To help with that effort, I have created the following chart. Remember, these are simply guidelines to consider; you will need to tailor your specific opportunities according to your own desires and requirements.

WHAT MILLENIALS VALUE	WHAT YOU MIGHT PROVIDE
Collaboration	Team-based assignments and projects
Structure	Well thought-out tasks with definitive start dates and end dates; a formal internship orientation and conclusion process; scheduled meetings for evaluation and mentoring discussions
Risk-taking	The opportunity for creative problem-solving; the chance to use an "out-of-the-box" approach to complete a task
Technology	Opportunities that utilize the newest forms of technology; a laptop for the summer; the chance to learn new software
Social Networking	Invitations to client meetings and customer appointments; lunches out with members of your team; exposure to the "higher-ups" within your organization
Challenging Goals	Assignments that require students to learn something new, research a concept in-depth, or apply a theoretical principle
Diversity	The opportunity to work with many different members of your company in many different departments
Flexibility	A flexible work schedule; the opportunity to work from home (or on nights or weekends); the ability to choose the projects worked on
Concern for the Environment	Opportunities to recycle or to use recycled goods; a paperless environment; some time to volunteer for a local charity
Leadership	The opportunity to make presentations to other employees; the chance to run a meeting, organize an event, or head a committee

Sections adapted from *Connecting Generations: The Sourcebook* by Claire Raines.

PLEASE REMEMBER:

- ❖ Internships are no longer about getting coffee and making copies. Students want to work on challenging assignments that will make a real difference in the life of the organization.

- ❖ Job descriptions should meet the needs of both students and employers. They should provide a clear and honest description of opportunities that students find attractive and that employers deem necessary.

- ❖ Learning objectives will vary from student to student, but will generally fall into one of four categories: skill development, academic enrichment, career development, and personal enhancement. The objectives should be specific, measurable, attainable, realistic, and timely.

- ❖ Regardless of whether or not you play a role in developing the intern's learning plan, your goal as internship supervisor is to ensure that the assignments and projects you assign allow the intern to fully meet his or her objectives by the end of the semester.

- ❖ Today's students are part of the "millennial" generation, a group of individuals who are highly educated and hold high expectations for themselves, as well as, others. There are ways to carve out specific opportunities within your internship program that will uniquely appeal to these students.

CHAPTER SIX

MAKING THE GRADE: FEEDBACK AND EVALUATIONS AND ASSESSMENT, OH MY!

Ah, the wonderful world of assessment. The sweet sound of praise, the deafening din of criticism, the toils and tribulations of evaluations. We've all provided feedback and we've all received it, as well. And guess what? As an internship supervisor, you are in for an entire semester's worth of comments, advice, pointers, and remarks in response to your intern's progress toward his or her learning objectives, goals, and completion of assignments. This is a *good* thing, as you are helping to shape the career development of a young professional! Therefore, let's spend a few pages discussing how to best support your student's growth, through the use of both informal feedback and formal evaluations, over the course of his or her internship.

INFORMAL FEEDBACK

One of the most important facts that you have to remember throughout the internship is that your intern is a *student*. As such, he or she is a relative novice in the professional business world and does not have a particularly large (if any) frame of reference in which to operate. As a result, *your intern is bound to make mistakes*. Let me say that again: your intern is going to make mistakes. Most often, these mistakes will be rather small in nature and easily repairable. Nonetheless, as the intern's supervisor, you will need to address these errors in such a way as to make the student aware of what went wrong without causing unnecessary and undeserved stress (on both your parts). On the (much happier) flipside, your intern is, inevitably, going to do some really great things! During these times, you will want to bolster the student's self-esteem even more by lavishing praise upon, and paying tribute to, his or her skills and abilities.

How you manage this responsibility and dole out both criticism and praise is up to you and will depend upon your management style, communication preferences, supervisory comfort level, and day-to-day schedule. Some internship supervisors prefer to schedule weekly meetings where the past week's accomplishments can be discussed. Other supervisors prefer to meet with the intern on an as-needed basis. Still others prefer daily ten-minute "check-in" appointments to talk about the day's events. Again, it is your choice as to how you would like to provide both positive and negative feedback to your intern.

My own experience has led me to become a big fan of the "it's never too much" approach. I would check in daily with the interns under my supervision, meet with them weekly, and talk to them whenever an issue that warranted discussion presented itself. I had an open-door policy and was always available via email or cell phone. I would like to think that my interns were comfortable coming to me with questions and concerns, and that I provided them with an ample amount of both praise and constructive criticism which allowed them to grow, develop, and improve themselves over the course of the semester. Some of my students needed more attention than others, but, in general, they all tended to become much more self-reliant as the semester progressed, and I found that most of my comments usually revolved around praise for jobs that were very, very well done, indeed!

Remember, too, that as students, your interns are used to receiving immediate feedback on their work. Although the breadth and depth of this feedback will differ from professor to professor and from class to class, students are typically aware of how well they are doing, overall, as they progress from assignment to assignment. In other words, they are not (or should not be, despite what they may say) surprised at the end of the semester with how well or how poorly they have done. As their supervisor, please try to provide your interns with timely responses to their queries and immediate (or as close as you can get) reactions to their work. They will sincerely appreciate your awareness and sensitivity, and, as a result, you will reap the benefits of their gratitude.

FORMAL EVALUATIONS

Performance evaluations—love them or hate them, for better or for worse, we have all participated in them and, yes, you will have to complete them for your intern. I say "them" because, ideally, you will complete one evaluation during the mid-point of the internship and another evaluation at the end of the internship. Your company will, no doubt, have its own form for full-time employee performance evaluations, and it is fine to mirror your intern evaluation form after this one.

But, in addition, you might want to consider the following categories and/or questions that apply specifically to internship experiences:

SKILLS:

Communication Skills (oral and written)
Research Skills
Presentation Skills
Interpersonal Skills

Analytical Skills
Computer Skills

ABILITIES:
Getting along with others
Working in a team
Working independently
Meeting deadlines
Keeping supervisor updated and apprised of progress
Public Speaking
Working with clients

PROFESSIONALISM:
Dress
Work Ethic
Promptness
Office Etiquette / Protocol

I would also strongly encourage you to leave room for open-ended comments as well.

Questions to prompt these comments might include:

- ❖ What are my intern's strengths?
- ❖ What are the areas in which he/she can improve?
- ❖ What was my intern's greatest accomplishment and why?
- ❖ What advice would best assist my intern with achieving his/her career goals?

While you may choose to use the same form for both the mid-semester evaluation and the final evaluation, there are a few differences you will need to think about.

SOME KEY POINTS TO REFLECT UPON:

THE MID-SEMESTER EVALUATION:

- Completed during the mid-point of the internship
- Addresses performance up until this point
- May include a revision of learning objectives or goals for the rest of the internship
- Discusses ways to improve performance

THE FINAL EVALUATION:

- Completed during the last week of the internship
- Addresses performance throughout the entire internship, but may focus on progress during the second half of the experience
- Includes assessment of whether or not learning objectives and goals were met
- Discusses strengths and weaknesses of intern and may include recommended career/professional development advice

While these evaluations will most likely go into the intern's personnel file in your Human Resources Department, it would behoove you to keep a copy for yourself, since you never know when you might be requested to serve as a reference for a past intern. You may also be required to send a copy of the evaluation to the intern's school—if the student is participating in the internship for academic credit, the completed evaluation form is usually factored into the student's final grade for the experience. Additionally, it would be a nice gesture to provide a copy of the evaluation to the student for his or her records.

It should go without saying that it is expected of you to share both the mid-semester evaluation and the final evaluation with the intern. I often took my interns out to lunch to discuss their evaluations, but having a sit-down in your office is perfectly fine, too. As long as you provide the opportunity to discuss your assessment of the intern's performance with him or her, location isn't a huge factor. What is critical, though, is that you encourage a dialogue with the student. Give your intern the opportunity to agree or disagree with your evaluation. Ask for his or her feedback on your supervisory skills. Discuss how each of you can improve the next time around. Remember that you both have room to grow and develop, and encourage each other to share ways to make that happen. Simply put, no one is beyond improvement, and everyone likes to be praised. Remembering this will enable you to become one of the greatest intern supervisors ever!

PLEASE REMEMBER:

- Similar to your regular full-time employees, interns require as much, and sometimes more, feedback from you, both in terms of constructive criticism and praise.

- It is up to you to decide how to deliver this feedback, but daily or weekly scheduled appointments might make the process easier.

- Two formal (written) evaluations are usually standard within internship programs: one at the mid-semester point in the experience and one at the end.

- There are certain skills and abilities that student interns want to hone, and these categories might provide you with a structure for conducting the evaluations.

- Discussing the evaluation with the intern during a private face-to-face meeting will allow you to share ideas about how to make internships a win-win experience for both of you.

CHAPTER SEVEN

(AIN'T IT GOOD TO KNOW THAT) YOU'VE GOT A MENTOR

One of the greatest gifts you can give your intern over the course of the semester is the opportunity to develop a relationship with a mentor. Mentoring is a wonderful way to share knowledge about a particular career field and allows for a symbiotic professional relationship that can benefit both the student (mentee) and the business professional (mentor). For the student, mentors can provide exposure to an industry or field of interest. They can assist with general career advice, the formation of short-term and long-term goals, and specific job-related challenges. Having mentees, on the other hand, offers the chance for professionals to reflect on their own success, pass along their advice and counsel, and play a role in developing the next generation of workforce employees. While it is acceptable for you, as the intern's supervisor, to play the role of the mentor, it is also reasonable to assign another individual to this task. Either way, there are several key roles a mentor should be prepared to play.

These include: teacher, guide, role model, coach, friend, motivator, and doorman[1], and involve the following responsibilities:

As a TEACHER

Mentors should teach mentees the skills, abilities, and capabilities that are required to be successful in the role of intern. Knowledge shared should be specific (the organization) as well as general (the field).

As a GUIDE

Mentors should provide a means of traversing through the ins and outs of the organization, including negotiating red tape, politics, and unwritten rules.

As a ROLE MODEL

Mentors should uphold the professional standards, values, and ethics that are expected within the organization and within the industry. Mentors should be the "superstars" to whom we all aspire.

---

[1] Adapted from the National Institute of Health's Management Intern Program guidelines.

As a COACH

Mentors should help interns with strategies, tactics, and approaches for success. These "gameplans" should initially serve to guide mentees through the course of their internships and continue to prepare them for victory long after their departure.

As a FRIEND

Mentors should neither judge nor admonish mentees; instead they should listen, encourage, and inspire. Ideally, mentors should act as objective parties, providing a safe haven within which the mentee can explore, reflect, and muse.

As a MOTIVATOR

Mentors should provide support and encouragement to their mentees, especially during the beginning of the internship, as well as throughout the (inevitable) challenges ahead.

As a DOORMAN

Mentors should act as gate-keepers. Whenever possible, they should expose mentees to experiences that will broaden horizons, people who will offer opportunities, and situations that will provide for learning and enlightenment.

As most college students seek out internships to further explore career fields of interest and to gain exposure to and experience with different organizations in their field, it is important that they have a mentor to help guide them through this process. As mentioned earlier, the internship supervisor can easily serve as the student's mentor; however, there are distinct differences in the two roles. While the job of the supervisor is to manage the intern's work assignments and to critique and evaluate the intern's accomplishments, the role of the mentor is not that of a "boss". Instead, the mentor's role is to aid the intern in his or her professional development, in general. Additionally, the mentor does not involve himself or herself in the day-to-day activities of the intern. His or her concern is the longer term, strategic focus on the career development of the student. In short, the supervisor's interest is the intern's job and the mentor's interest is the intern's career.

While the internship supervisor should always feel comfortable acting as a mentor to the student, you may want to assign another individual to assume this role full-time. If you choose to select another individual to be the intern's mentor, it is important that you keep in contact with this person throughout the course of the internship and that you set expectations for him or her at the start of the semester.

The employee you select should possess a few key characteristics that will allow the mentor/mentee relationship to be as beneficial to both parties as possible. To begin with, the mentor you select should like working with college students. This sounds obvious, but sometimes the best mentor "candidates" aren't ideal choices because they don't have (or don't want to use) the time, energy, and patience that college students require. Also, the person you select should have a depth and breadth of experiences that he or she would be willing to talk about.

IMPORTANT POINT HERE:
These experiences do not necessarily have to be entirely within your company, or even within your particular field. The best mentors I have ever seen have a wealth of experience, both personal *and* professional in nature, that they are more than willing to share (in the hope that someone younger will mimic the good experiences and avoid the bad ones)! It is hopefully obvious at this point that the mentor should be a good communicator, as well as a good role model. Other traits that are important for mentors to have are: objectivity, honesty, credibility, assertiveness, compassion, and tolerance. By far, the most important goal is to create a secure environment within which the mentee can feel comfortable sharing information, ideas, thoughts, and beliefs, asking questions, and addressing concerns with a respected and trustworthy partner.

In thinking about whom you might select to mentor your intern, keep the interests of your teammates in the back of your mind as well. Mentoring offers the opportunity for professionals to pass on their wisdom, hone their communication, interpersonal, leadership, and management skills, and learn from the youngest members of the workforce (who typically have fresh outlooks and new ways of thinking about things). In my experience, mentors are nearly always grateful for the opportunity to coach a more inexperienced individual and they often come away from the experience with a sense of personal gratification for assisting the "next generation" of workers.

Because mentoring is a less formal process than supervising, the actual "business" of mentoring can happen anywhere and everywhere. Of course, more formal meetings can be scheduled—for example, coffee, lunch, or dinner meetings. An easy way to proceed is to have the mentor and mentee arrange standing weekly, bi-weekly, or monthly appointments. These appointments may cover specific topics or can just be informal chats. It is really up to the mentor and mentee to decide upon what arrangement works for them. Examples of topics to discuss (with the mentor sharing his or her personal experience) might be: how to begin a career in the field, how to deal with and overcome difficult challenges, what advice might be most valuable for someone just starting out, what the industry code of ethics dictates, and how to work with difficult clients. One of the best ways to commence a mentor/mentee relationship is by asking the student what he or she wants to get out of the relationship. One student may want the opportunity to observe and interact with employees out in the field, another student may ask for feedback and advice, a third student may need simple encouragement or championing, and yet the last student may want to gain practical skills and abilities.

A WORD OF CAUTION HERE:
A mentor is not expected to solve problems, rectify situations, and/or fix mistakes. That is the job of the intern's supervisor. In the case of a mishap, the mentor's role would be to work with the student to reflect upon what happened and provide the intern with support, encouragement, and information so that the student will have alternatives in mind for the future.

As a mentor, you or your appointed designee will help your mentee grow by imparting knowledge and information via anecdotes and stories, role modeling, and active reflection. You will provide both a source of comfort and an answer to questions. Your insight into situations, both personal and professional, and your ability to look at a situation as an objective third party will enhance your intern's understanding of the world and will allow your student to build a solid foundation upon which to create future successes. Whether your particular role at any given time may be advisor, advocate, coach, teacher, counselor, role model, or doorman, you will always be to the student, in a single word, a friend.

PLEASE REMEMBER:

- ❖ Mentoring can benefit both the mentor and the mentee.
- ❖ Mentoring is different from supervising, although the internship supervisor can play both roles if desired.
- ❖ Mentoring involves (informal) teaching, guiding, modeling, coaching, supporting, and motivating, the specifics of which depend on the mentee.
- ❖ Mentoring may involve casual chats, scheduled appointments, or both.

CHAPTER EIGHT

AND NOW A WORD FROM OUR SPONSOR, SOCRATES

As an internship supervisor, you may, at some point, find yourself having to address issues that border on the unethical. Whether the intern is intentionally being deceitful (doubtful), or simply lacking good judgment (probable), you may potentially find yourself in an awkward and uncomfortable situation. For serious offenses like theft or violence, of course, you would want to call in your Human Resources Department immediately. Be assured, this very rarely happens. But, for other, less severe infractions, you will want to address the intern directly.

Now, ideally, as part of your company orientation, you would have already addressed the rules and regulations of your organization, along with matters such as dress code standards, confidentiality procedures, etc. Perhaps you would have even talked about such matters as respect, fairness, compassion, trustworthiness, citizenship, and responsibility. After all, the best way to handle any type of ethical or judgment dilemma is to avoid its occurrence in the first place. Still, it is important to remember that while college students are technically "adults", they do not have the perspective and experience that other workforce employees have. Therefore, there will sometimes be situations that arise that require your intervention.

Let's take a look at some of the issues that have developed as a result of internship experiences and briefly discuss how they might be addressed.

Your company sponsors a Friday evening happy hour. Upon arriving, you see your (under 21) intern happily chatting with other co-workers while enjoying a nice cold beer.

Yikes! What a way to put a damper on the evening! If the happy hour is on the company premises, you are absolutely obligated to address this situation since your organization is liable and at risk. Keeping things somewhat light, you might want to casually saunter up to the intern, pull him or her aside, and say something like "I'm glad you decided to come tonight, and it's nice to see you here, but shouldn't you be drinking water or soda?" This will get the message across (in a non-confrontational manner) that you know that the intern is under age and, legally, not allowed to partake in the alcoholic part of the festivities. At the same time, you are not suggesting that the intern leave, nor are you making a big scene causing undue embarrassment and ridicule. The student will get the message and the party can continue as planned. The same method of addressing this issue would apply even if you were not on company property.

You hear your intern engaging in inappropriate talk (sexual, racial, etc.) with a co-worker or client.

I can actually speak from experience on this one. I once had an intern who shared a love of, shall we say, "explicit internet media content" with another employee in our firm. Now, in all fairness, it was our employee who was completely out of line by initiating the conversation with our intern (he was eventually fired), but for a few weeks before anyone found out the nature of their discussions, they enjoyed sharing stories and, sometimes, even pictures(!) with each other. I only found out about this when I walked into the employee's office and saw and heard things I never thought I would encounter in the workplace! Immediately, I took the intern into my office and explained that, although I understood that he was approached by our employee and did not instigate these inappropriate discussions, under no circumstances were topics such as this to be discussed in a place of business. He explained that he was somewhat uncomfortable as well, but did not think that anything was egregiously wrong since the employee was a senior level member of our staff. It did not help that our intern was in the process of completing a major assignment for this employee and did not want to do anything that would jeopardize his success. I chalked this up to naivety on the part of the intern; nevertheless, we talked for approximately an hour about professional business conduct and what to do if he ever found himself in such a tricky situation again. To be clear, I did not blame the intern in this case. However, I felt it necessary to speak with him about the experience so that he would not make a similar mistake again.

It is advisable to obtain guidance from your Human Resources Department on the policies and codes of conduct regarding any kind of harassment including racial, sexual, and physical. Although harassment should never be tolerated, college students have a very different culture and their own unique code of ethics where off-color jokes, potty talk, and social behavior are concerned. Comments that they may not blink twice at may cause you, as a supervisor, to blush. I have lost count of the number of "f-bombs" I have heard during my conversations with student interns over the last several years because they have become too numerous to keep track of. Are these students trying to be offensive? Certainly not. They simply don't know any better (although, perhaps, they should)! So, while it is imperative to address any witnessed or reported inappropriate talk or conduct, keep in mind that, while some behavior may indeed by the result of malice, most behavior will, inevitably, be the result of ignorance.

Your female intern comes to a client meeting dressed in a shirt way too low-cut, a skirt way too high, and thigh-high boots that, while stylish on the runways of Milan, don't exactly conform to the conservative dress code standards your company upholds.

(Alternatively: Your male intern comes to a client meeting in wrinkled khaki pants, untucked button down shirt, and sneakers with nose ring and eyebrow piercings in full view.)

Again, this issue was most likely already addressed during the orientation process, but it will probably need to be revisited at least one more time during the semester. Students have their own version of what is considered business attire, and that version does not necessarily correspond to reality (go to any university job fair and you will see for yourself). You will need to address the student in a tactful, non-threatening manner and explain that the preferred style of business dress for your organization (client meeting, etc.) is such-and-such. If you are dealing with an intern of the opposite gender, it may be more comfortable for you to have a team member of that gender approach the student in your place. Encourage the student to ask you questions and, if time permits, have the student spend some time with one of your team members who exemplifies the "style" to which the student should aspire. This example doesn't fall under the realm of ethics, but it does involve professional acumen and judgment, two areas where college students sometimes fall short.

You pass by your intern's desk and hear him or her talking on the phone to a friend about matters that are confidential in nature.

This is a very severe (although, most likely, innocent) infraction, and one that might put your organization at serious risk. If your company deals with information that is private or proprietary in nature, chances are you had your intern sign a confidentiality agreement at the start of the internship. If you did not require this, now would be a really great time to do so! If the intern has already signed such a document, it would be best to re-address the terms of the agreement and stress to the intern that, although you are quite sure he or she meant no harm, it is vital that the information to which he or she is privy remain secret. I have never heard of an intern deliberately violating the terms of such an agreement, but I have heard of interns sharing information without truly understanding why such public broadcasting was wrong. Explain to your intern the potential harm that could befall your company should client or company information become fodder for public consumption; chances are the student will be extremely apologetic and not breach your trust again.

In general, my personal opinion is that students who participate in internships are typically quite mature for their age. These students tend to be intelligent, honest, trustworthy, and respectful. However, that does not mean that they are also not naïve in some respects. If you keep in mind their lack of experience in the professional work world, it becomes obvious that the occasional lapse in good judgment is accidental and needs nothing more than a quick face-to-face conversation to make things right. It goes without saying that, as their supervisor, you should be setting a good example for your interns by promoting integrity, dignity, accountability, fairness, and compassion in all that you do. While not necessarily a direct learning goal of an internship experience, an added bonus for students would be the knowledge that they are confident in their ability to recognize, manage, and resolve whatever "questionable" situation may come their way.

PLEASE REMEMBER:

- ❖ College students sometimes make errors in judgment that need to be addressed.

- ❖ These errors are primarily due to a lack of professional work experience, but may have ethical ramifications.

- ❖ The best way to address these lapses in judgment is by bringing the problem to the intern's attention in a non-threatening, non-confrontational manner and educating him or her on the situation and the resulting consequences.

- ❖ It is important to address (or re-address) your organization's business code of conduct and emphasize to the intern that he or she should come to you with any and all questions or concerns regarding workplace behavior.

CHAPTER NINE

IT'S THE END OF THE INTERN WORLD AS YOU KNOW IT (AND, HEY YOU ACTUALLY FEEL FINE!)

Congratulations! You have made it to the end of your semester, and both you and your intern are prospering. Pat yourself on the back for a job well done! However, you still have one more very important task to complete before you call it a semester. You must "end" the internship. I know. It is kind of strange to think of "ending" something in the active sense of the word, but, alas, there are steps that you need to take to successfully conclude the experience. Specifically, let's talk about how to do this by examining how to:

1) acknowledge the last days of the internship,
2) conduct an appropriate exit interview, and
3) arrange for plans to follow-up and keep in touch.

SAYING GOODBYE

Assuming all went well during the internship (as I'm sure it did!), you might want to consider hosting some kind of formal event to signify the conclusion of the experience. A very simple yet meaningful gesture is to sponsor a farewell lunch with the intern and your team during the final week of the internship where your employees can acknowledge and recognize the student's contributions over the course of the last few months. This type of celebration can involve brief presentations, anecdotes, and/or musings from individuals who worked closely with the intern over the semester. Students typically like to be the center of attention, and this type of recognition is usually well received. If you wish, you might ask the intern to prepare an overview (including, perhaps, a final project, presentation, or portfolio) of what he or she learned during the experience and share it with the group. Reflecting upon the experience will help the student to internalize the learning and skills he or she has developed and will enable you to provide a sense of closure to the internship. The key here is to keep things light and fun. Although you want the student to feel like he or she has "owned" this experience and is coming away from it a better, stronger, more enlightened individual, you do not want to make this culminating celebration feel like yet another pressure-filled, stressful assignment for which he or she will be critiqued.

Some organizations will have the capability to convert the intern to a full-time employee directly at the end of the internship. Others will be able to make the intern an offer of full-time employment later on down the road. Still others will not be able to do either, instead offering the intern nothing more than a wonderful letter of reference and a well wishes for any and all future endeavors. All of these scenarios are perfectly acceptable *so long as they are stated clearly at the end of the semester.*

The last week of the internship would be the time to discuss any or all of the following:

A job offer:
You would make the offer as you would for any other full-time employee, complete with title, job description, and salary/benefits information.

Instructions on how to pursue full-time employment in the future:
You would need to specify clear next steps, definite timelines, and application procedure.

Sincere gratitude for a job well done:
You would thank the student for all of his or her hard work and effort. As a nice gesture, you might want to offer to write a letter of recommendation, or at the very least, offer yourself out as a reference.

Again, any of these options are acceptable as long as the student is presented with clear and concise information.

CONDUCTING AN EXIT INTERVIEW

Exit interviews are often used by Human Resources Departments to capture specific organizational information from departing employees. Data gleaned from these discussions often help companies revise and improve their business practices. In order to evaluate the effectiveness of your internship program and/or position, it is critical that you employ this practice with your student upon conclusion of the semester. In addition to providing a sense of finality to the internship (for both you and the student), an exit interview will allow both of you to reflect upon the experience in an effort to assess how beneficial it was to each party. The feedback you receive from the student will help you and your organization find ways to better support and accommodate student interns in the future. Exit interviews with interns may also reveal a wide range of opportunities for improvements in organizational business policies, procedures, and systems.

It is very important that the exit interview (or "discussion", if you prefer) remain informal and casual. The tone should be conversational in nature. Your goal is to create an environment where the student will feel free to discuss his or her thoughts. This is not the time or place for an interrogation. If at all possible, you, the intern's supervisor, should be the individual who conducts the exit interview. Not only will you be more likely to understand the intern's comments (from an organizational perspective), the intern will probably be much more comfortable stating his or her feelings directly to you since, ideally, you will have developed a level of trust over the last few months.

My personal experience with intern exit interviews is very positive. During the many years I was involved with college recruiting, students never ceased to amaze me with their exceptional insight and their unique perspective regarding business matters. The relatively "green" students, lacking any real professional business experience, were able to talk about the way things "should" work (in their view of the ideal fantasy workplace). While not entirely practical on all accounts, these students often pointed out real inadequacies in a workplace that too often relied on the "status quo" method of getting things done. The more experienced students, with one or more previous internship experiences under their belts, were able to compare and contrast our business environment with others in which they worked and offer both praise and criticism in equal amounts. The insight of these students was very helpful to me.

While you are encouraged to keep this conversation relatively relaxed, it would certainly behoove you to provide some sort of a structure to keep the discussion focused and on target.

Here are some examples of questions you might consider incorporating into your chat. Feel free to provide a copy of the questions you would like to discuss to your student in advance, so that he or she has adequate time to brainstorm, compose his or her thoughts, and participate in this discourse effectively.

- ❖ Did this internship position meet your expectations?
  Why or why not?

- ❖ Did this internship experience succeed in relating to your academic major and/or career goals? Why or why not?

- ❖ Do you feel that your assignments were helpful in meeting your learning goals and objectives? Why or why not?

- ❖ Did you obtain a clear picture of the career possibilities within this organization? Why or why not?

- ❖ How do you feel that this experience has affected your future goals and/or influenced your perspective on the industry/field/profession?

- ❖ Did you feel respected and valued as a member of our team? Why or why not?

- ❖ Do you feel that the supervision you received was adequate? Why or why not?

- ❖ What did you enjoy most about your experience?

- ❖ What did you enjoy least about your experience?

- ❖ What comments or suggestions can you offer to help make our a) company stronger and b) our internship program more effective?

- ❖ Would you recommend our company to other students as a place to intern? Why or why not?

Keep in mind that exit interviews are only as effective as you make them. In other words, you must be willing to actively listen to the student's ideas and probe for more information. Don't let them get away with the "everything was great!" comment. Ask for details, solicit examples, and obtain clarification when necessary. Think of your student as a (cheaply paid!) consultant. You would not ask a consultant to "sugar coat" the truth, so why not encourage the student to provide candid, honest responses to your questions? It can only help you the next time around. An open-minded supervisor sincerely committed to workplace improvement will ask, listen, ask some more, respond accordingly, and seriously consider the information presented. Done well, the exit interview can provide you with a wealth of information that is crucial to helping your company and internship program grow and prosper.

KEEPING IN TOUCH

If I had a nickel for every time I told a student to "keep in touch! keep in touch!

keep in touch!" with networking contacts, former supervisors, past professors, family friends, etc., I would be immensely rich, retired, and sitting on a beach drinking piña coladas right about now. And yet, now I am going to say it again, to you, the internship supervisor. I am even going to put it in italics and bold for additional emphasis:

Although the internship is officially over, you would be very wise to keep in touch with your (now former) intern throughout the following year.

This applies to interns who have received a job offer, who may receive a job offer, or who did not receive a job offer (because you could not offer them a job, not because their performance did not warrant one). You want to make absolutely sure that you ask the student for his or her forwarding information, both phone number and email, before he or she leaves. Your goal in doing this is to ensure that the relationship you have developed with the student remains strong throughout their final year (or years) in school. Why? Let's look at the following scenarios:

1. You have offered the student a position and he or she has accepted

Great! Fantastic! Congratulations! Wait a minute, though. There is almost an entire year between now and the date the student would officially start as a full-time, permanent employee. Hmmm...isn't there a fairly large on-campus recruiting program at the student's school? Aren't there other companies who do the same thing you do? And have better benefits? And pay more? And offer more exciting opportunities? Truth be told, despite the fact that students are told, time and time again, to never renege on an accepted offer, it occasionally happens. Keeping in touch with the student throughout the course of the following academic year will not necessarily prevent something like this from happening, but it can make it less likely. (From a former college recruiting manager whose company hired upwards of 300 summer interns a year, trust me on this one.)

2. You have not offered the student a position yet, but plan to later on down the road

Wonderful! You already have a (potential) head start on filling your recruiting pipeline. But again, your organization is one of many competing for top talent. Don't think that your intern is not checking out all of the other fabulous opportunities available to him or her. In this scenario, you must continue to "woo" your intern throughout the year or else risk losing him or her to another company. Remember, memories only last for so long, and the loving feelings that your intern has towards your company in September may quickly fade by the following February if no effort has been made by you in retaining the student's interest.

3. You did not offer the student a position because there was no opportunity to do so.

No open positions right now? Not a problem. But, given the recent instability of the economy and the workforce, who is to say that things won't change on a moment's notice? Keeping in touch with the student not only connects you to him or her, but also connects you to other students whom your intern knows (and who may be better fits for the types of opportunities that do, eventually, open up). The most successful headhunters know that, when speaking to a job candidate, you should always end your conversation with "Who else do you know?" or "To whom can you refer me?" The same principle applies when working with students. They are connected to, literally and figuratively, hundreds of other students (ever look at a college student's MySpace or Facebook page?!) and students talk. Therefore, keeping in touch with your intern, despite the fact that there are no current opportunities available, is a smart thing to do for any potential recruiting you may have to do in the future.

There are several ways in which you may choose to keep in touch with your intern. Some actions require more time and effort than others, but any of them are perfectly acceptable and will accomplish your goal of maintaining at least some form of contact throughout the following year. Regardless of the approach, it is important that you communicate on a regular basis so that your organization is never far from the intern's mind.

Here are some tried and true methods for you to consider:

- ❖ Send cards – holidays, birthdays, good luck on finals
- ❖ Send food – candy for Valentine's Day and Halloween, pizza for exam week
- ❖ Send (or email) the company newsletter or a monthly update about new projects and/or people

- ❖ Invite the student back for company gatherings – picnics, sporting events, holiday parties

- ❖ Establish a company presence on a social networking site and include the student as a friend

- ❖ Sponsor a campus event, preferably one in which the student participates

- ❖ Offer to have the student work at your company part-time or during breaks in school, or bring him or her in to contribute to a special project

- ❖ Continue the mentoring relationship by having monthly lunches together

- ❖ Pick up the phone randomly and call to say hello

Another idea that deserves mention is one that has been used successfully by larger organizations for quite some time. The theory is this: students who have interned within your company (and who have had great experiences) will be able to help you in your recruiting efforts by helping to convince *other* (top) students to find out more about available opportunities within the organization. These programs are sometimes called "ambassador" programs because your former interns act as good will emissaries, spreading positive press about their experience as an intern. Some companies choose to compensate their former interns for this work, others do not. Those that pay usually require the intern to conduct a more formal marketing campaign. The recommendations that the student ambassadors make can easily lead to increased interest amongst the student body and can greatly save you both time and money in recruitment costs. One of the reasons these programs are so successful is because students tend to listen to other students more carefully than they listen to most anyone else. Students appear more credible and more believable than recruiting professionals or Career Services representatives and, therefore, the information they provide holds more weight. Another reason that ambassador programs work well is that students are extremely knowledgeable about their school's unique culture and communication mechanisms and understand exactly when, where, and how to tap into the best student talent. Whether in student groups and clubs, classes, extracurricular sports, or online, great students will attract and interact with other great students, which means a self-generating target market of exceptional students, all for you!

So, although it may be time to say goodbye to the internship, it is not at all time to say goodbye to the intern. Properly ending the experience by commemorating its success and providing the opportunity to share and collect information is a necessary part of concluding the internship, but keeping in touch with your intern and maintaining contact throughout the upcoming year will serve you well in the months to come.

PLEASE REMEMBER:

- ❖ Ending the internship is just as much a process as starting the internship and should be planned out in advance.
- ❖ It's nice to formally conclude the internship with a special lunch or party. This makes the student feel special and allows other employees in your organization to express their thanks.
- ❖ Let the intern know what to expect in terms of a future position with your company, and clearly and specifically delineate any relevant next steps.
- ❖ Conducting an exit interview will enable you to solicit helpful feedback about your internship program and will permit your intern to share his or her ideas for improvement.
- ❖ Remaining in contact with your intern over the following academic semester and/or year is a smart idea as it will allow you to further develop your relationship with the student as well as increase your organization's exposure to other top students on campus.